The Imagination
in the
Modern World

BY STEPHEN SPENDER

*Three Lectures Presented Under the
Auspices of the Gertrude Clarke Whittall
Poetry and Literature Fund*

REFERENCE DEPARTMENT

THE LIBRARY OF CONGRESS

WASHINGTON : 1962

62-64964

L.C. Card No. 62-00000

FOR SALE BY THE SUPERINTENDENT OF DOCUMENTS, U.S. GOVERNMENT
PRINTING OFFICE, WASHINGTON 25, D.C. - PRICE 25 CENTS

THE GERTRUDE CLARKE WHITTALL
POETRY AND LITERATURE FUND

The Gertrude Clarke Whittall Poetry and Literature Fund was established in the Library of Congress in December 1950, through the generosity of Mrs. Gertrude Clarke Whittall, in order to create a center in this country for the development and encouragement of poetry, drama, and literature. Mrs. Whittall's earlier benefactions include the presentation to the Library of a number of important literary manuscripts, a gift of five magnificent Stradivari instruments, the endowment of an annual series of concerts of chamber music, and the formation of a collection of music manuscripts that has no parallel in the Western Hemisphere.

The Poetry and Literature Fund makes it possible for the Library to offer poetry readings, lectures, and dramatic performances. Each year a series of lectures is devoted to a common theme. These three lectures, which were delivered on February 26, 27, and 28, 1962, are published by the Library to reach a wider audience and as a contribution to literary history and criticism.

Contents

The Imagination as Verb

THE SITUATION OF THE POET is certainly a topic much discussed at literary conferences. Often, the discussion takes the form of poets' telling a large audience that they cannot communicate with its members. Sometimes, it takes the more practical one of discussing how to give economic aid to poets by making them do other things than write poetry—teaching, for example. Anyway, it offers a picture of poets as being peculiarly helpless in the circumstances of modern life.

The question "What can poets do to save civilization from destruction?" is often asked by some member of the public at the very conference where the poet is on show in his role of helpless, hopeless anachronism. This suggests that poets, though neglected, somehow command the secret of the time in which we are living. If the Voice of the Imagination were heeded, enemies would be reconciled and the hungry fed. Two confusions are involved here. One is that there is a tendency for the poet to be more a matter of concern than the poetry. The other is the idea that if poetry and the poet were given their true place, this would really have some effect on a world distracted and tormented with fear. This second proposition is one that poets—that is, imaginative writers (whether they write poetry, fiction, or drama) sometimes share.

The belief that poets can alter and have altered the world is contained in Shelley's famous claim that poets are the unacknowledged legislators of mankind. No modern poet would regard this as anything but preposterous. Yet underneath the denials, the idea that the life and works of the imagination somehow provide an incandescent center in which human personality and even social forms can become molten and transformed certainly persists in Lawrence, in Rilke, even in Joyce.

So much preoccupation with the situation of the poet and with the function of the poetic imagination results doubtless from the feeling that, in the past, poets fitted better into the community, and their poetry was better understood. Certainly, we are right in feeling that there was a difference, but I doubt whether this was it. There were perhaps merely different expectations on the part of the poets, different misunderstandings on that of the public. What may be a modern peculiarity is that poets today expect to be understood for the qualities they regard as intrinsic to their poetry being poetry, just as painters expect their paintings to be admired not for their subjects or their beauty but for qualities called painterly, perhaps even for the texture of the surface of the pigment.

No one could say that the poets of the Victorian era—Tennyson, Browning, and Arnold—were neglected or even went unappreciated. And yet they seem rather like displaced persons who enacted to their audience the Victorian public's idea of "the poet," rather as a refugee may, in his exile, find himself having to act out the accent and behavior which his neighbors expect of someone coming from the country of his origin. "Vex not thou the poet's mind, With thy shallow wit," Tennyson growled at a public expecting the cloaked and bearded poet to growl. And if one glances back rapidly from precedent to precedent of English poets across the centuries, one finds poets who were courtiers, cavaliers, politicians, customs inspectors, ambassadors, writers of flourishing dedications to patrons, lunatics, and gangsters, but rarely a situation which could be regarded as favoring them simply because they wrote poetry. This is true even of the greatest. We feel that Milton belonged to the conscience of a puritan revolution (though he had friends who were poets and scholars), that Shakespeare belonged to a very fertile period in history and a group of players, that Chaucer was one of his own Canterbury pilgrims, that Wordsworth was the property of the Wordsworthians, that the Romantics belonged to their biographies, that Tennyson belonged to Arthur Hallam and Queen Victoria.

If we are discouraged by the thought that modern poets don't "communicate," we may find comfort in the reflection that there have been few periods when their poetry communicated *as poetry*. In the opinion of his contemporaries, Shakespeare seems to have been only one among a number of playwrights who were doubtless judged not for the poetry but for the play being the thing. He comes rather low on the list of playwrights supplied by his contemporary, Meres.

Yet I would not care to dispute the truth of the observation of someone who said that a modern poet, launching forth his slim volume of verse today, is like someone dropping a feather over the edge of the Grand Canyon and then waiting for the echo. Nevertheless, certain living poets get back a considerable reverberation. We ought to remember this. What is more important, there never was, as I have written above, a period in which the arts were more appreciated for the specific qualities that are considered peculiar to each of them. In fact, the arts run the risk of being overpurified and the artists of feeling obliged to produce some quintessential extract of the qualities of their art, so great is the pressure of critical connoisseurs on them to produce only the real, right thing.

It is really as though, in an age of specialization, poetry only has to communicate along the pure packed line which Keats, reproaching Shelley, said should be "loaded with ore." This means that we do ask ourselves "Is this poetry?"; where in the past people might have asked: "Does it tell a story?" "Does it praise the king?" "Has it a moral?" "Does it conform to the standards which we call beautiful?"

Poetry is an end, where previously it was often regarded as a means, a vehicle for carrying flattery, beauty, melodrama, religion, a moral, or just the world. And this situation seems acceptable to some poets, notably Robert Graves, who draws the logical conclusion that poets should write only for other poets and should take in one another's washing. In one of his early letters, Ezra Pound declares that a poet should not expect to find more than thirty readers who appreciate his work for its true qualities.

I do not take it for granted that poets today have a grievance. Nevertheless, we do feel—and rightly, I think—that whether poetry is admired for the wrong or the right reason, there is, as it were, a reduction of scale in its relation to a world of machines, scientific inventions, world power-politics. This diminution corresponds, perhaps, to the ratio of modern man to the almost annihilating scale of the time-space universe, of modern man even to his own inventions. There is, perhaps, not so much a breakdown of communication as a kind of shrinking of the imagining, the feeling, the flesh and sense tissues through which the poetic communicates, in relation to the great exaggeration of impersonal, inhuman forces.

Critics have offered many reasons for this state of affairs. Ever since Matthew Arnold, they have been telling us that there is a decay of the institutions which communicate values in society itself, and that therefore poetry cannot today become (using Matthew Arnold's own epithet, in his lecture on *The Function of Criticism at the Present Time*) "important."

It is symptomatic, perhaps, that in the late nineteenth century Arnold used the word "important" with regard to poetry, where we should probably write "significant." We avoid "important" because it sounds too public; "significant" can be as private as we want it to be. If you say an art is "important," you imply that there is a confluence of subject matter, interest, and values within the art, with things outside that are important by standards outside it. Our current use of the word "significant" can have no reference to anything outside the standards set up by the work itself, just as a symbol can, with the "Symbolistes," symbolize only itself. What was important to Matthew Arnold was important to Mr. Gladstone. Nothing that is significant to me is important to Mr. Harold Macmillan. So in using the word "significant" in modern criticism, we limit ourselves to that which is signified within the terms of the art, to the reader trained to receive what the poem communicates.

So, it has come to be accepted that what is significant along the channels of communication between poet and reader is not important in public thought. Poetry—and hence imaginative literature—has become "significant" when it has ceased to be "important." Poet and reader are inmates of the prison cell shared by Lear and Cordelia, when Lear has abandoned all power and most claims on life:

> *. . . Come, let's away to prison;*
> *We two alone will sing like birds i' the cage;*
> *When thou dost ask me blessing, I'll kneel down*
> *And ask of thee forgiveness. So we'll live,*
> *And pray, and sing, and tell old tales, and laugh*
> *At gilded butterflies, and hear poor rogues*
> *Talk of court news; and we'll talk with them too—*
> *Who loses and who wins; who's in, who's out . . .*

We accept the idea that there is an almost autonomous outside world of science, invention, and power, evolving and revolving according to laws of economics, etc., which has become unimaginable within the individual consciousness. This was not so for Shakespeare or Milton. Their imaginations roamed over the whole world and over the forces that controlled the history of their time. Here, surely, there is a real break between past and present.

The reasons for regretting the separation of the automatism of social forces from the shrunken inner worlds of individuated experience are not so obvious as might at first appear. The common misunderstanding started by Shelley is to regard the separation as a public catastrophe, as though poets might save civilization but are prevented from doing so by the forces of machinery and politics. It is not a catastrophe, and poetry cannot save nations, nor could it ever do so, though perhaps we should not overlook the capacity of poets in the past to create what politicians today call an "image." Virgil set out to create a pattern for Romans in *The Aeneid,* and Shakespeare (perhaps more successfully because less purposively) certainly created an "image" of England's country and soldiers, which perhaps helped to win the Battle of Britain. It certainly seemed incarnate in the few who won the cause of the many. Whitman, in *Song of Myself,* became the experiences of all America in order to provide Americans, in his self-portrayal, with a personalized image of America for which they might live.

We should all agree, though, that today poetry cannot save civilization. Nevertheless, to agree about this is not to argue that poetry cannot and should not make inner worlds of elements in the public world which are "important." There seems to be a tendency today to think that, in their poetry, poets should not reconcile outward things with inner life but should deal only with such things as are already inner, personal, private, or literary. One can sympathize with this tendency, which can become both stoic and playful in poems as excellent as those of Philip Larkin. Nor am I suggesting that there is some obligation imposed upon poets to be socially responsible, if I add that the mind which creates from imagination should be able, ideally, to imagine what seems impersonal, or even unimaginable.

[4]

If none of the contemporary poets is able to compose inner worlds that include elements of the public world—the world that was felt in *The Waste Land* as in Auden's *Spain*—then contemporary poetry reflects a partial failure to imagine the disturbing modern environment. The reader or aspiring young writer (over-impressed perhaps by C. P. Snow's *The Two Cultures and the Scientific Revolution* or concerned with the Bomb) may well find himself apparently confronted by a choice between the limited, private, personal, literary-academic world of the imagined and the abstract, threatening, open world of the unimaginable. There is the suspicion today that poetry is the playground of perpetual students—or perpetual professors—who have achieved their maturity at the price of refusing to have dealings with the world. Robert Graves, in answering a questionnaire, declared in *The London Magazine* of February 1962 that "personal issues are all that interest people, not newspaper issues," a statement which can only be taken to mean that Mr. Graves thinks that nothing of public concern, which is discussed in the newspapers, can be felt by the reader to be his personal concern. Since questions involving the survival of the reader and of his loved ones are newspaper issues, this seems an ostrich-like attitude. It also seems characteristic of a habit among modern writers of setting up false dichotomies between "public" and "private," "personal" and "impersonal." The contradiction between "personal issues" and "newspaper issues" disappears when one reflects that no newspaper issue is a subject for art unless it is felt by the artist as one affecting him personally—as the bombing of Guernica affected Picasso. In the past there was major and minor poetry but no idea that it was honorable for all poetry to be minor and poetically disgraceful to attempt the major themes of the whole of life viewed as a whole. There was no idea that the world of art was somehow the opposite of the world of historic action.

When Matthew Arnold set himself up as the advocate of the Function of Criticism, his plea (more influential than the one on another occasion that poetry might replace religion) was that "creative power works with elements, with materials," and that if these are not present, "it must surely wait till they are ready." In the present century, critics like T. E. Hulme, I. A. Richards, and T. S. Eliot have explained that the elements which are lacking are values and beliefs, fragmented and decayed in modern scientific and materialist societies. In some quarters, the decline of institutions in society upholding values and beliefs has led not so much to the view that criticism can prepare the ground for "important" poetry as that it must take the place of major creative effort by keeping open the connections with the past organic society of living values through the selection and analytic study of those works which are truly in the Great Tradition. The Great Tradition and the analysis of the values in these works replace both poetry and religion.

The view is that poetically we live in a vicious circle which completely conditions literary creation. There are no effective institutions of faith and values because there are not the faith and values, and there are not the faith and values for poetry to draw on because there are no such institutions. This vicious circle is also held responsible for the breakdown of communication in poetry.

This depressive analysis leaves out one thing. It does not explain why, until recently, there have been poets of the stature of Yeats, Eliot, and Frost writing great poetry. Moreover, it should be pointed out that this very habit of explaining the situation of poetry in terms of the collapse in values, itself shows one of the symptoms of the situation complained about—a desperate dependence on outward circumstances, a materialist tendency to explain the inner state of the individual artist as entirely the result of outward conditioning.

I think criticism has been too preoccupied with conditioning circumstances. It is inevitable that it should be so. Critics deal, after all, with things given, what is already written, what they find going on in the life around them, the already read, not the as yet unwritten. One of the things that creative talents do is change into favoring circumstances the unfavorable conditions out of which they create. Eliot, writing as a critic, easily demonstrates the impossibility of Eliot's writing *The Waste Land*. I cannot accept altogether the view that poetry is the result of analyzed circumstances. So what I have set myself to do here is to separate, for the time being, the idea of poetic imagination from the context of conditioning history, to consider it as an activity per se, to take it, as it were, out of the context of conditioning non-values.

Shakespeare wrote comparatively little about poetry. When he describes the process of making poetry, he suggests the operation of an independent creative faculty upon things immediately apprehended:

> *The poet's eye, in a fine frenzy rolling,*
> *Doth glance from heaven to earth, from earth to heaven;*
> *And as imagination bodies forth*
> *The forms of things unknown, the poet's pen*
> *Turns them to shapes and gives to airy nothing*
> *A local habitation and a name.*

The citation is so familiar and itself so airy, so Mozartian, that it slips by almost unconsidered. But what is said is surely astonishing: that the form of things remains unknown until the poet, standing midway at the center of his universe, bodies them forth; that the imagination is a pure activity, making named forms out of nothings.

It is noteworthy that Keats and the other Romantics returned to this Shakespearean view of the imagination as an independent sovereign activity, centered in the poetic genius and owing allegiance to no superior intellectual authority. In doing this, the Romantics rejected the practice of the Augustan poets, who put their great imaginative gifts at the service of theological, aristocratic, and rationalist-philosophic views of their times. Eighteenth-century poets like Pope considered the imagination to be the servant of the intellectual rationalizations of the age, which seemed to reconcile the reasoning of God with that of scientists. To the Augustans, poetry was an intellectual synthesis which, in its transparent imagery, had the ambition of resolving discords between different spheres of contemporary reasoning.

Keats returned to the view, which he discovered in certain passages of Shakespeare, that imagination is a primary faculty of the poetic sensibility, whereas fancy and wit are secondary, illustrating already conceived ideas. Imagination can be thought of as purely inventive, conjuring shapes out of nothing, or as the center of poetic sensibility acted upon by experiences. It receives these experiences and transforms them so they can be related one to another within the harmonious unity, the world in little, which is the poem. Imagination comes before intellectual concept, whereas wit or fancy or illustration demonstrate idea.

The Romantics rebelled against their predecessors, the Augustans, against the poets of wit, because in them the imagination had become adjectival, imaginative. The imaginative was put to the service of reason. The Romantics returned to the concept of the imagination as verb, the Word made flesh, the dream which is Adam's. As Coleridge wrote: "to contemplate the ANCIENT of days with feelings as fresh, as if all had then sprung forth at the first creative fiat."

The great revival of interest in Shakespeare which we find in Blake, Wordsworth, Coleridge, and Keats was a return to the Shakespearean as source in English poetry of primary imagination. The Romantics bring us back to the idea of poetic imagination as dreaming yet revealing consciousness, in which the circumference of brute facts, experiences, and disparate ideas becomes self-aware and, in the moment of self-awareness, is transposed into symbols and images harmonious within the complex unity that is the poem.

Ideally, the circumference comprises the whole world of knowledge, experiences, and events, past and present, which are undigested in the sense that they can only be interpreted into the significance of inner life through the power of the imagination to relate them within the unity of the poem. The force of Shelley's *A Defence of Poetry*, which remains impressive—however many holes may be picked in his argument—is his vision that, ideally, the real world is material potentially capable of being transformed by the imagination. He realized, too, that the world—in its most ancient history as in its most recent inventions—is always contemporary consciousness, coming alive within the awareness of individuals living at a particular moment, people having the attitudes of their generation, their situation in time and place.

[7]

Shelley, in his view of poetry, was of course concerned with an ideal, not with a program that could be laid down for poets. He was writing of a desideratum, not of what was necessarily within the capabilities of his contemporaries, when he wrote in 1820:

> . . . The cultivation of poetry is never more to be desired than at periods when, from an excess of the selfish and calculating principle, the accumulation of the materials of external life exceed the quantity of the power of assimilating them to the internal laws of human nature. . . .

Here, imagination is regarded as the transforming center of poetic consciousness, a task, and perhaps a body of contemporary achievement above and beyond any individual poet "imagining that which we know" for his generation, as task and sum of scientific knowledge stand beyond the individual scientist.

In spite of the reaction today against the Romantics, modern poetry and criticism have taken over the view of the imagination as center, acted upon by experiences and inventing its own harmonious inner world; and, in spite of talk of a revival of classicism, they have not returned to the essentially classical view that imagination is the power of illustrating theology, monarchy, or philosophy, dressing up, as it were, preconceived ideas about the important values of living. Baudelaire was anti-Romantic, theologically minded—yet he regarded the imagination as standing above the experiences on which it operated:

> The whole visible universe is but an array of images and signs to which the imagination gives a place and relative value; it is a sort of fodder which the imagination must digest and transform. All the faculties of man's soul must be subordinated to the imagination, which can call upon them all at once.

Coleridge, in one of the most famous passages of *Biographia literaria,* defines imagination as "the power in which one image or feeling is made to modify many others, and by a sort of fusion to force many into one."

And, in a still more famous passage:

> The poet, described in ideal perfection, brings the whole soul of man into activity, with the subordination of its faculties to each other according to their relative worth and dignity. He diffuses a tone and spirit of unity, that blends and (as it were) *fuses,* each into each, by that synthetic and magical power, to which I would exclusively appropriate the name of Imagination. . . .

In the present century, at a later stage of modern poetry, imagination begins to be regarded as arbiter in a world of fragmented values, or, in the thought of Rilke, as the molten memory of traditions which have vanished from the world, in Yeats as mouthpiece of the "images in the Great Memory Stored." Rilke is perhaps the twentieth-century poet most seized with the idea of the poet having a task of fulfilling the past so that it redeems the present. In doing this, imagination becomes the force in which memory of traditions which once gave living significance is reinvented. In a letter to

Witold von Hulewicz explaining the purpose of his *Duineser Elegien,* Rilke writes:

> The Elegies show us engaged on this work, the work of the perpetual transformation of beloved and tangible things into the invisible vibration and excitability of our nature, which introduces new "frequencies" into the the pulsing fields of the universe. . . . And this activity is sustained and accelerated by the increasingly rapid disappearance today of so much of the Visible which we cannot replace. Even for our grandfathers, a house, a fountain, a familiar tower, their very clothes, their coat, were infinitely more, infinitely more intimate. . . . The lived and living things, the things that share our thoughts, these are on the decline and can no more be replaced. *We are perhaps the last to have known such things.* . . . The earth has no alternative but to become invisible IN US. . . ."

So Rilke regards the task of poetic imagination to be that of setting up a kind of machinery which connects the reinvented past with the present. The angels in the elegies might be compared to vast transformers standing above a human landscape, converting the energy of the divine and the traditional into power which flows over and redeems the banal life of the fair in the valley below, whose values are those of money.

Rilke's purpose calls to mind Matthew Arnold's suggestion that "religion . . . will be replaced by poetry." This idea has, on the whole, received a bad press from critics, especially from those, like Eliot, who think that poetic imagination should at some point fuse with impersonal authority, and who would reinforce authority with irrefutable dogma. However, Rilke could not accept the Roman Catholicism in which he had been brought up. For him it was clear that poetry is not so much a replacing of religion as a path hewn out, leading back to that in religion which is not dogma but imagined idea. "For poetry," writes Arnold, "idea is everything," whereas "our religion has materialized itself in fact, the supposed fact." But religion is, at some point, imagination identical with idea, and the attempt of the *Duineser Elegien* might be defined as that of tracing back both poetic symbol and religious belief to the place where the Word is flesh.

In an essay, *An Anatomy of Orpheus; Rilke Among the Critics,* Michael Hamburger cites several authorities to show that Rilke did in fact attempt to make his poetry a substitute for religion. To F. R. Leavis there is no question that D. H. Lawrence's message is "religious." Yeats makes a mosaic of fragments of Oriental and Western beliefs and varieties of mysticism, a religion as eclectic as the picture of art, selected from all times and places, which André Malraux, in his *Le Musée imaginaire de la sculpture mondiale,* supposes modern men and women to carry round in their heads.

So, although Arnold's idea is in disrepute among critics, it is to some extent prophetic of the development of modern poetry. When Arnold wrote that religion had "materialized itself in fact," he was doubtless thinking of the Victorian controversy between the religious and the evolutionists of his time over the origins of man. What has happened since is that the exaltation of the act of the creative imagination as a visionary or intuitive judging of the values of life in a civilization of fragmented values has, as a first stage, separated the imagination from current orthodoxies and brought it back to the idea of religion as imagination in action, creating the world. That "art creates values" was an idea frequently expressed by writers at the beginning of the present century. And the point I want to emphasize is that, although the view of poets having become dogmatically religious seems completely opposed today to that of the heretically undogmatic, the disagreement is in fact more apparent in their critical prose views than in their poetic imagination. Michael Hamburger gives some striking quotations from Wallace Stevens to show how close his attitudes are to those of Rilke:

> The poet has 'immensely to do with giving life whatever savour it possesses. He has had to do with whatever the imagination and the senses have made of the world. . . .'
> 'The world about us would be desolate except for the world within us. . . .'
> 'The major poetic idea in the world is and always has been the idea of God. . . .'
> 'After one has abandoned a belief in God, poetry is the essence which takes its place as life's redemption.'

This expresses the loneliness of the artist with his creation. It is the attitude of Henry James and of Joseph Conrad, which greatly influenced the early Eliot, and what I am suggesting is that it remains the attitude of modern poets in the actual creation of their poetry, and if they have reintroduced the idea of dogmatic religion, it is as corrective to what is dangerous and nihilistic in such an isolated imagination; but their reintroduction of dogma into their thinking is not a return to the kind of religion for which Arnold thought poetry might become a substitute, the religion "materialized . . . in fact." Dogma is to them not the center out of which they create but as a disciplining of the imagination. Dogma is to the pure imagination that which critical sense is to technical performance.

In the same article, Michael Hamburger observes that "religious faith is one thing, poetic imagination another," and the distinction he makes is that "faith demands a concentration of the will, whereas will is the enemy of imagination." This seems a bit baldly stated, since there have been, without their suffering inner contradiction, religious imaginative poets. Perhaps, though, in ages of belief, the inner imagining of poets is corrected by the surrounding discipline of an external will to believe. Thus, when Coleridge writes of the imagination as though it were a completely self-sufficient mediator between different faculties of the soul, he takes for granted that in acting thus it has already been influenced by ideas of "worth and dignity." In a time of disbelief, there is a danger of art's resulting from altogether uncontrolled imagination, from a surrender of the poet to his perhaps destructive and diabolic fantasies. For this reason, Eliot and

Auden distrust the heresies of the imagination which has become a value to itself. Nevertheless, to say that the religion of T. S. Eliot and W. H. Auden is the contrary of the irreligion of Lawrence and Rilke is to set up a false opposition. Religion in Eliot's poetry may involve insistence on dogma and traditional attitudes, but it is not a return to the religion that seemed unacceptable to Arnold. Indeed, in its imagining of mystical situations outside the temporal order, it might appear to Arnold to have some of the characteristics of poetry substituting for religion. In Eliot imagination remains the primary activity, just as it is in Yeats, or Rilke. Dogma has been introduced not at the center of the inspiration but as a principle of correction of extravagant despair or eclectic invention.

In the letter to his Polish translator already quoted, Rilke goes on:

> If one makes the mistake of applying Catholic conceptions of death, the Hereafter and Eternity to the Elegies or Sonnets, one isolates oneself completely from their conclusions and becomes involved in a fundamental misunderstanding. The angel of the Elegies is that Being in whom the transmutation of the Visible into the Invisible, which we seek to achieve, is consummated.

For Rilke imagination was, as it were, an acted-upon instrument played upon by traditional symbols and exposed to the modern environment. His sensibility—deliberately weaned from the Catholicism of his childhood—was to him the channel whereby religious symbols could become poetic ones, and his religious attitudes evolve within his poetry.

First Eliot and, much later, Auden supported orthodox Christianity, as converts, and in their stated views. But whereas Eliot's dogmatic faith seems to distinguish him sharply in his life and intellectual attitudes from a poet like Rilke (and still more from a Christian heretic like D. H. Lawrence), in *Four Quartets* and the *Duineser Elegien*, their *poetic* attitudes are not opposed. In the long run, and despite Eliot's earlier attacks on him, even Eliot and Lawrence meet in their having religious imaginations. It would be far truer to say that in the *Four Quartets* the poet uses theology and dogma in order to release his mystical imagination, than to say that he uses his imagination to illustrate his dogma. Perhaps Auden sometimes falls into a kind of Christian classicism—but this is where he is most willed and least convincing. Rilke, the non-Catholic but with his Catholic upbringing, uses his angels, saints, and dead souls much as Eliot uses sanctified places. The central experience of the *Four Quartets* is the pure imagining of ecstatic and mystical states of awareness—timeless within time, the striving of prayer towards identification of the self with the past of ritual.

*　*　*　*

What is common to these views—and I think to all major attempts in modern writing—is the view of imagination. The imagination has been restored in modern literature to its position of Verb. The reinstating of imagination as primary, central, the verb, was perhaps the attitude responsible for the greatest modern achievements: works like the last novels of Henry James (particularly *The Golden Bowl*), Joyce's *Finnegans Wake*, Yeats' Byzantium poems, and the *Duineser Elegien* put these writers in the God-like position of being isolated within their own creations, of having to reinvent the world and all its values within their art.

It is now possible, perhaps, to reconsider the problem of communication today in a way that is not the stereotype of sociological and analytical critics. As I remarked earlier, many of the misunderstandings which poets, and critics for them, complain about seem to have been always true of their situation, although it becomes clear that today an ancient problem takes special form. For example, I suppose it has always been true that poets and other artists are isolated. But in the past this has only been so in the sense that others also are alone. Shakespeare seems able to rely on the fact that the situation of Hamlet or Lear going to his doom is, in its essential relation to the human condition, only an extremely conscious and developed example of what each member of his audience might feel. The peculiar modern nightmare is that the artist appears to be working under circumstances in which he is not only solitary in his exceptional awareness of the human condition, but he is, as it may seem, alone in being alone. He is operating on an awareness of being alive in a world where people are encouraged in every way to identify themselves, not with the other people around them, all trapped in the same human situation, but with a whole machinery of getting through life, which distracts them from the fact that they are spiritual animals. This produces the special kind of modern incommunicability. If you are a poet, often you are talking about things which are real to you and which have been real to people in the past, but to which many contemporaries appear to have deadened themselves, assisted in the deadening process by all the machinery of advertising and distraction.

At this point there appears to be a failure of nerve, and a demand on the part of writers that they should return not to their humanity but to the traditional institutions which have, as it were, knocked into people's heads the situation of living a shared awareness as it was in past times; hence the return to dogmas and establishments and critical interpretations of past literature, the insistence on the selected volumes of the Great Tradition and their accompanying exegeses as Holy Writ. I wonder, though, whether the flight from creative into critical attitudes, which has been so much a feature of the past two decades, is itself not an escape from the main reality to be faced—the common fact of the humanity of each of us isolated within his modern situation. The point I am laboring is put far better in Joseph Conrad's *Heart of Darkness*, that work which seems to go further than any other into the implications of modern materialism. When Conrad's narrator, Marlow, has gone far into the jungle of the Belgian Congo (the passage has the significance of prophecy realized today)—with his dehumanized fellow explorers, who, in their search for ivory, are driven to their own deaths and to mass-murdering natives—he hears through the jungle the great roar of the savages who, concealed from the white traders, have been watching their approach. Suddenly he sees these hordes:

> . . . They howled and leaped, and spun, and made horrid faces; but what thrilled you was just the thought of their humanity—like yours—the thought of your remote kinship with this wild and passionate uproar. Ugly. Yes, it was ugly enough; but if you were man enough you would admit to yourself that there was in you just the faintest trace of a response to the terrible frankness of that noise, a dim suspicion of there being a meaning in it which you—you so remote from the night of first ages—could comprehend. And why not? The mind of man is capable of anything—because everything is in it, all the past as well as all the future. What was there after all? Joy, fear, sorrow, devotion, valour, rage—who can tell?—but truth—truth stripped of its cloak of time. Let the fool gape and shudder—the man knows, and can look on without a wink. But he must at least be as much of a man as these on the shore. He must meet that truth with his own true stuff—with his own inborn strength. Principles won't do. Acquisitions, clothes, pretty rags—rags that would fly off at the first good shake. No; you want a deliberate belief. An appeal to me in this fiendish row—is there? Very well; I hear; I admit, but I have a voice, too, and for good or evil mine is the speech that cannot be silenced. . . .

It seems to me that we have paid too much attention to the circumstances that condition the creating imagination. We lament the breakdown of beliefs, the decline in traditional values, the havoc wrought on civilization by the mass media—all these things—which add up to what we call the breakdown of communication. In painting ourselves as products of our social conditioning, we have not paid sufficient heed to the common and continuing human condition, the shared existing and experiencing within differing environments which is the real basis of communication.

If it is true that the poet today experiences alienation, it may also be true that there is a humanity of the nonliterary which he partly ignores. There is the poet, situated perhaps at the university; his loyalties and special interests are those of the literary group and his mental picture of the world is one of modern people whose attitudes he views as the results of the mass culture which is the worst enemy of his poetry. He regards his poetry as conditioned because he regards this public as conditioned. He only regards those who have critical consciousness, who are immersed through their reading and writing in values outside the contemporary ones, as being liberated from conditioning. But it may be that this picture of a public wholly conditioned by advertising, television, etc., is at least partly false, and that the literary intellectual's view of his isolation may be due to his having cut himself off from those equally aware of their human situation but as little able, in the circumstances created by his elite culture, to communicate with him as he is with them.

The difference between the poet with a view of catastrophe isolated in his literary consciousness, and the same view when it is an agonized state of consciousness shared with other lives, may be demonstrated by comparing two major works written out of the mood of World War I; these are *The Waste Land* and that little-known masterpiece, *In Parenthesis,* by David Jones. It does not make any difference to my argument that *In Parenthesis* is written in a style which owes something to Joyce and Eliot and that it is by a Roman Catholic. The point is that *In Parenthesis* celebrates communication of awareness, as the result of a common suffering, between the consciousness which is that of the poet, and that of the group of soldiers which it concerns. Both Eliot and David Jones see the same modern scene of the physical collapse of Western civilization. But the characters of the bank clerk, the secretary-typist, the pub-talkers in *The Waste Land* are psychological stereotypes projected by the surrounding moral chaos. In *The Waste Land,* it is only the consciousness of the poet, the sensibility realized in the poem, that expresses its awareness of a situation in a landscape in which all the other characters are unconscious, products of circumstances, lay figures. The characters of the soldiers in *In Parenthesis* become aware through that realization which is the result of having to act in the circumstances that were the Western Front: "the 'Bugger! Bugger!' of a man detailed, had often about it the 'Fiat! Fiat!' of the Saints." Thus, the soldiers are redeemed through the awareness revealed in their acceptance of duty and suffering into the writer's vision of Arthurian legend, Shakespeare's histories, and the offices of the Roman Catholic Church—just such values as are absent from the "young man carbuncular" in *The Waste Land.* But the soldiers walk in light:

> *Every one of these, stood, separate, upright, above ground,*
> *blinkt to the broad light*
> *risen dry mouthed from the chalk*
> *vivified from the Nullah without commotion*
> *and to distinctly said words,*
> *moved in open order and keeping admirable formation*
> *and at the high-port position*
> *walking in the morning on the flat roof of the world*
> *and some walked delicately*
> *sensible of their particular judgment.*

In Parenthesis celebrates the redemption of the soldiers, not the poet's awareness of them conditioned by circumstances which make redemption impossible to anyone except, perhaps, the poet.

Reading recently in *The Hudson Review* a selection of letters from German soldiers in Stalingrad, I had again the impression that where men are made aware of the extremes of the human condition in many cases the values whose loss the intellectual critics have so long deplored emerge. For those values are, at least in part, not institutional and doctrinal but potential in human individuals. What we lack more than values is awareness (when we are not by nature serious or made serious by being thrust into extreme situations) of what it means to be alive. But we can have faith that people are capable of being made conscious. I cannot believe that the decay of the "organic community" has deprived people of the potentiality to be awakened to the implications of consciousness.

By this I do not mean that the creative imagination must work upon that kind of chill contemporary humanism which is sometimes served up as the lowest common denominator of science and lost beliefs. What I do suspect, though, is that dogmas and orthodoxies are no way round the fact that in modern conditions all we can be sure of *knowing* is the common humanity of those who consider themselves civilized and those who howl and make faces on the shore. Beyond this, every "belief" is "deliberate" and deliberated. If it rests on institutions and dogmas, then those only divide it from the modern environment. Where it links up with others is in the common human need for affirmation from which it derives. That this is so is demonstrated, I think, not by current critical attitudes but by the greatest poetic achievements of our time which, in spite of dogma and orthodoxies, have rested on the idea of the liberated, unconditioned imagination.

I suggest that Yeats and Eliot and Lawrence and Faulkner, in spite of the fact that they themselves were traditionally-minded artists who deplored the breakdown of tradition in the life around them, clung nevertheless to the idea that the imagination must in modern circumstances reinvent values. It is the contradiction between an eighteenth-century, almost classical critical awareness and artistic self-consciousness, and this trust in the miracle-producing resources of the individual imagination, to which we owe the great achievements of modern art. There is danger today of the paradox being forgotten.

The Organic, The Orchidaceous, The Intellectualized

WE CAN HEAR THROUGH POETRY and criticism of the past 150 years a note of regret already poignant in Wordsworth and Coleridge. It is in Wordsworth's *Intimations of Immortality* in lines such as:

> *What though the radiance which was once*
> * so bright*
> *Be now forever taken from my sight,*
> *   Though nothing can bring back the hour*
> *Of splendour in the grass, of glory in the*
> * flower. . . .*

For Wordsworth, this hour belongs to the poet's childhood. But we feel that before Wordsworth's day it belonged to a life in harmony with poetry. The note is taken up by Coleridge in *Dejection: An Ode:*

> *But now afflictions bow me down to earth:*
> *Nor care I that they rob me of my mirth;*
> * But oh! each visitation*
> *Suspends what nature gave me at my birth,*
> * My shaping spirit of Imagination.*

The regret is for a period of innocence in which environment, existence, and poetic expression formed a single harmony.

This vision of childhood is celebrated, also, in Blake's *Songs of Innocence* in poetry of a spontaneous, seemingly still childlike kind. It is significant that the *Songs of Innocence's* "opposite" (to use the word in the Yeatsian sense), the *Songs of Experience,* embraces evil as the price paid in order that the poet may continue to experience life as existential:

> *'Love seeketh only Self to please,*
> *To bind another to Its delight;*
> *Joys in another's loss of ease,*
> *And builds a Hell in Heaven's despite.'*

It is as though Blake thinks that for the adult the childhood immediacy can only be retained by seeking evil in experience where the child found good. The view was expressed, with a sophistication which Blake would probably have disliked, by Baudelaire in *Les Fleurs du mal.* The world of Newtonian science and of "the dark satanic mills" which Blake saw emerging substracts the qualities that are personal and immediate from human relationships. Instead of innocent contact with good, or guilt-ridden but still personal contact with evil, there is, like the fogs of that black country of industrialist barracks which Blake saw covering the green English countryside, the screen between man and man of depersonalized values of power and materialism. Later poets have felt envy for poets preceding the industrial revolution, whom they believe to have lived in the presence of those forces of nature which are today screened from us as much by the inner processes of abstract thinking as by the outward appearances of industrial civilization.

Twentieth-century criticism is full of sophisticated attempts to explain what has been lost—the once associated forms of a sensibility now become dissociated, the pattern of living of the "organic community." But there is the possibility that the sophistication hides a nostalgia just as heavily romanticized as that of Thomas Carlyle for monastic life in the eleventh century, or William Morris for Merrie England. Eliot looks back to the Elizabethan age as "a period when the intellect was immediately at the tips of the senses. Sensation became word and word sensation."

From Carlyle, Ruskin, Morris, and Arnold to T. E. Hulme, Ezra Pound, Yeats, Eliot, Lawrence, and Leavis there is the search for a nameable boojum or snark that can be held responsible for splitting wide apart the once-fused, being-creating consciousness. The Renaissance, the puritan revolution, the French Revolution, the Industrial Revolution, have all been named as villains. There runs through modern criticism the fantasy of a Second Fall of Man. The First Fall, it will be remembered, had the result of introducing Original Sin into the world of Man, exiled from the Garden of Eden and knowing good and evil. The Second Fall seems to result from the introduction of scientific utilitarian values and modes of thinking into the world of personal choice between good and evil, with the result that values cease to be personal and become identified with the usefulness or destructiveness of social systems and material things.

Just as I tried before to separate the romantic concept of the power of the sovereign imagination from the picture given by critics and sociological analysts of poets writing in a society where their works are conditioned by modern circumstances, now I want to consider the idea of organic poetry as something separate from the conditions which are held to have produced the dissociation of sensibility.

I do not know whether it is possible to define organic poetry. But it should be possible to cite examples of poetry in which "sensation became word and word sensation," and to indicate the tendency of poetry to be organic in the work of poets who aim at this quality. Poetry tends to be organic when the words and form of the poem seem to grow out of the poet's experience of his environment, particularly, I should say, when that environment and experience seem "natural." There is a continuous process as from environment, through the poet's sensuous nature, into words and form. This is surely what Keats means when he says that poetry should grow as naturally as the leaves of a tree. By growing he does not mean that poets should not work, but that the work itself should resemble the process of diligently growing rather than intellectualization.

Organic poetry is, then, that in which there is identification of the poet's experience of nature (meaning by this the life around him sensuously apprehended) with the words used, without the feeling that mental activity falls like a shadow between the experience and the realized words and form. In such work, sensibility is sensuous, and if there is idea, then it also is experienced sensuously. In the poetry, the reader feels himself present with articulated life realized like leaf or flower by the words.

It is the quality in the speeches of Shakespeare's characters which caused Dryden to comment: "All the images of Nature were still present to him, and he drew them, not laboriously, but luckily; when he describes any thing, you more than see it, you feel it too."

The simplest and clearest examples of organic poetry are, perhaps, to be found in certain passages of Shakespeare's sonnets, for example, Sonnet 12 which contains the lines:

> *When lofty trees I see barren of leaves,*
> *Which erst from heat did canopy the herd,*
> *And summer's green all girded up in sheaves,*
> *Borne on the bier with white and bristly beard. . . .*

It is impossible, I think, to apprehend these lines except as the identification of the object with the feeling clothed in the language. It is as if one were standing in a harvest field with great trees very close and felt within the ripeness of the single moment the turning of all the seasons of the year, and as if at the same time this sensation was clothed in words directly springing from it. Intelligence and feeling are realized in sap and leaves.

Nineteenth-century attempts to produce a similar effect show the contrast between organic poetry and writing which, marvelous as it may be, springs not from immediacy but from the straining of memory after immediate effect. An example is the famous stanzas of Tennyson from *In Memoriam:*

> *By night we linger'd on the lawn,*
> *For underfoot the herb was dry;*
> *And genial warmth; and o'er the sky*
> *The silvery haze of summer drawn;*

And calm that let the tapers burn
  Unwavering; not a cricket chirr'd:
  The brook alone far-off was heard,
And on the board the fluttering urn:

And bats went round in fragrant skies,
  And wheel'd or lit the filmy shapes
  That haunt the dusk, with ermine capes
And woolly breasts and beaded eyes;

While now we sang old songs that peal'd
  From knoll to knoll, where, couch'd at ease,
  The white kine glimmer'd, and the trees
Laid their dark arms about the field.

This certainly paints a picture in the mind's eye. It is, indeed, a word painting; that is to say, it attempts in words what a painter does in his different medium. One art is skillfully used to suggest another. The words are chosen with conscious painterly precision and put on the paper at the brush's tip. "Underfoot the herb was dry." One savors the choice of *herb*. It is distinguished from *grass*, and at the same time contains the French word for grass. One may wonder whether in the recollected instant of regret for Hallam there is not too much observation in the "woolly breasts and beaded eyes" of the bats. The fact that the scene is dusk when one could not see "beaded eyes" suggests that the visual mind is working too hard. Too much meticulously detailed emotion seems to have been recollected in too much tranquility.

If, indeed, organic poetry was produced in nineteenth-century England, it is to be found, perhaps, not in the poets but in painters such as Samuel Palmer in his early watercolors and drawings, Constable in his sketches, and, above all, Turner.

The lines from Sonnet 12 which I have quoted might be taken as purely descriptive. It could be argued that they have something of the Wordsworthian approach to nature in that they are, perhaps, recollected from childhood; in the most English of meadowy, tree-weighed, river-woven landscapes, one imagines the boy Shakespeare standing in the ripe fields. But Sonnet 26 has the same quality of potent innocence, here embodied in thought removed from immediate observation:

Till whatsoever star that guides my moving
Points on me graciously with fair aspect,
And puts apparel on my tatter'd loving,
To show me worthy of thy sweet respect. . . .

In some of his later poems, Yeats celebrates the purity, strength, and sweetness which seem inseparable from lives lived passionately, in surroundings identified with vision handed down from the past. He praises those who have the aristocratic view, who live in the country, in great houses, inherit ancestral properties, ride to hounds, fish, are not "intellectuals." But he does so out of an awareness of his own divided being, torn by regret, filled with remorse:

> *Through intricate motions ran*
> *Stream and gliding sun*
> *And all my heart seemed gay:*
> *Some stupid thing that I had done*
> *Made my attention stray.*
>
> *Repentance keeps my heart impure;*
> *But what am I that dare*
> *Fancy that I can*
> *Better conduct myself or have more*
> *Sense than a common man?*
>
> *What motion of the sun or stream*
> *Or eyelid shot the gleam*
> *That pierced my body through?*
> *What made me live like these that seem*
> *Self-born, born anew?*

Yeats makes a sharp distinction between the life that is a poem, and the sedentary, reflective, remorseful, and nostalgic life which is that of the poet writing poetry. The life that is a poem unreflectingly fuses environment with living. It is the life of people who have not thought and who therefore, if they are privileged, can go on living as their forebears did. But this is impossible for the modern poet, who must needs be reflecting, responsible, remorseful, conscious of a fate of the world wider than the sphere of life he might sensuously apprehend. There is much regret in Yeats for a time when, as he thinks, it was possible to be poet, scholar, and gentleman. So where in Shakespeare there was the unity of unconscious being with conscious creating, in Yeats there is an almost bitter admiration for the "dumb" life of uncreative full-blooded action, bitter regret that the poetic occupation has barred him from poetic existing:

> *I leave both faith and pride*
> *To young upstanding men*
> *Climbing the mountain-side,*
> *That under bursting dawn*
> *They may drop a fly;*
> *Being of that metal made*
> *Till it was broken by*
> *This sedentary trade.*

*   *   *   *

What is called Nature poetry began with the industrial era. With the covering over of the countryside by the industrial slums, untouched nature became a spiritual value. The deeper significance of Nature poetry is surely that it was the attempt of certain poets to return to organic poetry by placing themselves within a setting from which they rejected the values of their contemporaries, those of the town, and put them back into the period of history which belonged to the countryside. The movement from London to the Lake District was not just a geographical withdrawal. It was also a retreat into a fortress of past time. It is significant that Wordsworth, in the introduction to the *Lyrical Ballads,* is not just concerned—as the Wordsworthians sometimes seem to think—with natural scenery and picturesque peasants. He was also concerned with *natural* people—those who lived in Cumberland, their behavior and view of life, and the language they used, which he felt should be the idiom of poetry, because it was the idiom of lives in contact with nature. They were not the lives of the town.

Wordsworth identified the nature of Windermere and Derwentwater with his own childhood. He sought to recover a fusion of nature and being, which he once enjoyed, by reliving those surroundings in his poetry. His greatest descriptive passages have kinetic energy. "Kinetic" is defined in the *Shorter Oxford English Dictionary* as "the power of doing work possessed by a moving body by virtue of its motion." When Wordsworth is actually walking, in motion, literally with muscles and mind going over the territory of his childhood, his memory functions intensely, and his poetry communicates re-lived physical sensation and spiritual exaltation with correspondence of word after word to footstep after footstep. *The Prelude* is the first great *A la recherche du temps perdu.* What is being recaptured is not just the poet's own past but the past relationship of English poetry to the natural environment. And if the Nature poetry of the lake poets is a reaction against industrialism—against the nineteenth century—it is also a reaction against the urban poetry of Pope—against the eighteenth century—whose poetry, in its ideas, was the instrument of a rationalist aristocratic elite.

Augustan poetry was illustrative then of attitudes toward life, theses, rationalism, social hierarchy, fashions, belonging to that age, to the mentality and intellectual life of the town. Wordsworth turned away from the town to seek out the sources of being and feeling as against those of will and reason. This choice is clear enough. The child cannot distinguish between its own body and its mother's, inner self and outer world. It is this sense of returning to an almost pre-conscious level which results in an ambiguous vagueness when Wordsworth attempts to restate his sensations as a philosophy of the unity of being and experiencing:

> . . . . *a sense sublime*
> *Of something far more deeply interfused,*
> *Whose dwelling is the light of setting suns,*
> *And the round ocean, and the living air,*
> *And the blue sky, and in the mind of man* . . . .

Here is the *idea* of the organic, but it is not organic in expression.

The ode on *Intimations of Immortality* is one of the great poems in the English language. Having said this, one might well add that it is both profoundly unsatisfactory as communicated innocence and profoundly unconvincing as philosophy. It opens with the poet's recollections of the time that was when the earth seemed "apparelled in celestial light," the light of a glory which has now passed away from the earth. In his childhood, the poet both saw and was one with what he saw. Today, he looks, and things are as beautiful as they were, and yet they remain outside him, they are not an inseparable part of his own being. The being-creating fusion has been split apart. He attributes this calamity to his exile from his own childhood. The view of life he offers to justify the intensity of childhood experiences seems taken for granted by Wordsworthians. It has not always aroused sufficient amazement. It is usually accepted, I think, as belief in reincarnation, and Indians are pleased to think that it provides one of those occasions when English poetry links up with Oriental philosophy. Actually, it puts forward a theory of pre-incarnation, in which we are invited to look backward to a state of existence precedent to birth but not forward to later incarnations. The title, indeed, fits strangely with this view, which suggests that impressions grow ever fainter as our days distance from the mystical state before birth. There is no indication that posthumous intimations will be stronger than the pre-natal ones, unless perhaps we are to suppose that they precede later births. But this is unlikely, since the pre-natal experience is not represented as being posthumous to a previous life. In fact, any given moment of consciousness is the faintest, because the last, in a line of impressions ever weakening as they grow further away from pre-natal bliss:

> *Our birth is but a sleep and a forgetting:*
> *The Soul that rises with us, our life's Star,*
> > *Hath had elsewhere its setting,*
> > > *And cometh from afar:*
> > *Not in entire forgetfulness,*
> > *And not in utter nakedness,*
> *But trailing clouds of glory, do we come*
> > *From God, who is our home. . . .*

We are asked, here, to share the feelings of a consciousness which laments the loss of its unconsciousness but which at the same time romanticizes unconsciousness, as a peculiar and intense state of consciousness, of organic union with the mystical sources of nature. The objection to this is obvious— that unconscious bliss only exists at the moment when it becomes conscious, and that Wordsworth never entered into the full innocence of being a child until he wrote this poetry. All the same, this answer does not entirely cover the case. For childhood in his poetry is also a metaphor for a world in which there is no divorce between feeling and creating.

Coleridge, in his *Dejection: An Ode,* analyzes more prosaically the split between childhood joy and adult awareness, between consciousness and unconscious nature. He admits that it is our own consciousness which gives unconscious nature its attributes:

> *O Lady! we receive but what we give,*
> *And in our life alone does Nature live:*
> *Ours is her wedding garment, ours her shroud!*

What is true of nature is also true of childhood fused with its surroundings. Wordsworth "creceived"—to use Coleridge's word—his childhood because he realized it through his adult consciousness by means of the poetic gift in which that memory was more aware. Coleridge goes on:

> *And would we aught behold, of higher worth,*
> *Than that inanimate cold world allowed*
> *To the poor loveless ever-anxious crowd,*
> *Ah! from the soul itself must issue forth*
> *A light, a glory, a fair luminous cloud*
> *Enveloping the Earth—*

Here, the accusing finger points, the boojum is named. It is the "inanimate cold world" with its "loveless ever-anxious crowd" and its material goals and debased values, the urban consciousness, which has set a barrier between the abstract aims of living and "joy," "the shaping spirit of the imagination." It is this which has thrust the poets and "the happy few" (as Stendhal named them) back upon their own resources, so that they must create out of themselves the luminous values which may still envelop the earth.

Coleridge thinks that he might—as he believes Wordsworth succeeded in doing—win back that unity of inward being with outer nature which makes it possible to write organic poetry, the line that springs directly from "the shaping spirit of imagination," which is the result of world-excluded "joy." And certainly the characteristic of the greatest passages in *The Prelude* is that the language and the thought expressed become one with the sensation experienced.

For later poets, what may seem enviable about the lake poets is that they were living in an early phase of modern history when it was still possible for them to reject industrial civilization and choose natural scenery as though it were an alternative which met the life of the town on equal terms, without too much sacrifice of significant expression. Of course, there have been poets since who have rebelled against industrial society— D. H. Lawrence did. But despite his hatred of the towns, Lawrence thought in the idiom of the Nottingham of the coal mines and the chapels in which he had grown up; and the "nature" which he invoked against the industrial urban consciousness had much more of rebellious instinctual human nature about it than of natural scenery, the moods of the weather, and the annals of the peasantry.

Historically, Wordsworth was the last poet who, making such a choice, could write great poetry. This is perhaps to put the matter too crudely; but at the stage of the industrial revolution that was Wordsworth's youth the country and the town life might still have seemed in balance, just as Blake's protests against science and rationalism still had the force behind them of a time when it might have been possible to choose a path other than the one that led to the "dark satanic mills," to reaffirm the England that was Blake's Jerusalem. But, already in the mid-nineteenth century, for a poet to have devoted himself to writing about the scenes and experiences of his childhood in the countryside would have been to write poetry about things that no longer seemed to constitute "important" experiences in the history of modern civilization.

The scene of the larger battle for writing poetry about the human condition in modern times had to be transferred to the towns and the preoccupations of people living in the world of industry and science. Yet, the lake poets defined a choice which still remains between organic, imaginative writing and that which Lawrence called "cerebral," but for which—since cerebral seems denigratory—I prefer to use the term "intellectualized."

That which to Wordsworth was nature was to Keats the poetry of Chaucer, Spenser, and Shakespeare, his deliberately sought-out environment. His was a life lived as far as possible as poetry. Everything in his letters points to his intention of living in the world as though it were palpable poetry, everything in his poetry to his determination to regard his poetry as surrounding life. "Oh, for a life of pure sensation!" he cries, meaning by this not what the editor of the *Chicago Tribune* or the London *Daily Express* might mean, but that he wished to live in a continuity of a sensuously apprehended experience which was one with the sensuous experience of the poetry he read and wrote. In his poetry there is a tendency to identify experienced sensation with sensation imagined, to think that if he could not live a life that was poetry, then he could inhabit a poetry that was life. He recounts the experience, apparently frequent with him, of being rapt from the actual world—the anatomy lesson at the medical school where he was an apprentice—to a far realer world of poetic imagining. What he expected from his friends—Reynolds, Hunt, Shelley, and the others—was that they should form a magic circle which would exclude nearly all experience except the life of the imagination. The kind of reality which makes us call certain novelists realists was to Keats a stiletto pointed at the ruby jugular vein of lived dream. His identification of beauty with truth was simply a way of stating his lived identification of imagination with a passionately sought-out reality. In the context of his poetry and letters, what he meant by "Beauty is truth, truth beauty,—that is all/ Ye know on earth and all ye need to know" is so clear that it is difficult not to suspect critics of bad faith when they pretend not to know what it means.

In his uncannily perceptive study of Keats, Middleton Murry shows the extent to which Keats identified his poetry with the Shakespeare of *Romeo and Juliet, A Midsummer Night's Dream,* and *King Lear.* What corresponds in Keats to the pre-natal Wordsworth "trailing clouds of glory," is a pre-natal Keats who was the young Shakespeare. We are often told that Keats wrote "pure poetry." This is true if we mean by it that he invented lines which, while remaining original to him, were yet a concentrated essence of Chaucer, Spenser, Shakespeare, and Milton become his own spiritual habitat. But such quintessentialized poetry is not the same thing as what I call organic poetry, which springs directly from nature and life. Murry almost convinces himself—as he convinced me when I was 17—that through identification the 23-year-old Keats *was* the young Shakespeare. Beware! Such identification results in extreme dissimilarity to the person with whom one is identified. Shakespeare, himself, was Shakespeare and not identifying with, say, Chaucer. Keats' poetry, like the poetry of Walter de la Mare, fed off other poetry and the idea of poetry. It is exotic, parasitic, orchidaceous. However, sometimes—through the veils of his own and other men's dreams—experience poignantly personal to him, a real anguish, a real love which refuse to be fobbed off with the poetic, break through and become disturbing autobiographic poetry.

What I have been trying to show is that at the beginning of the Industrial Revolution and until our own day, two interconnected things have happened, which have had revolutionary effects on imaginative writing. One is that poets have felt threatened by a change in consciousness from organic and concrete to scientific and abstract thinking. This has cut them off from a past when poets were intimately and, as it were, immediately in touch with the sacramental, the personal, and the natural forces that were once the ritual of living. The other is that, as a result of this sense of an irremediable change, there began to be an examination and re-evaluation of the once-primary place of imagination in life as in poetry. Although there has been a reaction against the Romantics, there has been no return to the idea that the imagination could or should be put at the service of a rationalistic or politic view of life.

Nostalgia for organic poetry, in which the poetic flows, as it were, in an interrupted continuum out of living experience causes perhaps the bitterest reaction of the modern poet to life as it has been since the Industrial Revolution. It may seem curious that this is so, since organic writing makes up only a small proportion of past literature. It is rare even in Shakespeare's sonnets. Shakespeare usually uses the devices of intellectualized poetry in the way in which a modern poet would. He constructs, for example, metaphors from the machinery of the law to demonstrate his complex feelings about his relationship with a friend. The irony with which, in Sonnet 87, the friendship that is of feeling, without calculation, based on genius, nature, and generosity to the poet, is recognized as being calculated and contractual on the part of the young man, is also modern:

> Farewell! thou art too dear for my possessing,
> And like enough thou know'st thy estimate.
> The charter of thy worth gives thee releasing;
> My bonds in thee are all determinate.
> For how do I hold thee but by thy granting?
> And for that riches where is my deserving?
> The cause of this fair gift in me is wanting,
> And so my patent back again is swerving.

Organic poetry, as I have attempted to describe it, arises out of an assumed harmony not just between man and his fellow beings, not just between man and social institutions, but between man and the forces in physical nature, perhaps the nature round him, perhaps his own instinctual nature. The supposition is that the powers, deriving from the star, the sap, the soil, reaffirm the natural order of society, the naturalness of human love. The feeling of nature, moving with the forces of stars and weather and beasts magnetically through individual life and through the social hierarchy, is very strong in *King Lear*. Rereading the play recently, I noticed how it is underlined by the character of Albany, husband of Goneril. He is, militarily speaking, on the wrong side in the conflict between the forces of Edmund and those of France. But it is he who abandons the cause of his wife when he sees that her and her sister's behavior is not just wrong but against nature:

> That nature which contemns its origin
> Cannot be bordered certain in itself.
> She that herself will sliver and disbranch
> From her material sap, perforce must wither
> And come to deadly use.

So passionate regret is expressed by Eliot for the period before the dissociation of sensibility, and by Yeats for a life in which there is no division between the "wise and simple man," "A man who does not exist/ A man who is but a dream"—the fisherman—and the poet, with his sedentary trade, which cuts him off from that time when he himself was of those who "drop a fly" "under bursting dawn." The bitterness is the sense that he is cut off because of the poetry; and yet he feels that in differing circumstances, the poetic imagination would have been entrance to that very sensuous being from which the poet, doomed to intellectualization, is now barred. It seems impossible today to think of the poet as Marvell did when he wrote in *The Garden* of a correspondence between being and creating like intellect complementary to nature:

Mean while the Mind, from pleasures less,
Withdraws into its happiness:
The Mind, that Ocean where each kind
Does streight its own resemblance find;
Yet it creates, transcending these,
Far other Worlds, and other Seas;
Annihilating all that's made
To a green Thought in a green Shade.

What seems to have been disrupted, then, is the being-creating fusion, where in participating in the resemblances which are nature, the poet also comes into possession of his own mind, and makes a fusion which transcends both nature and intellect.

The bitterness at the splitting of the being-creating fusion is, in Yeats, peculiarly personal, a special grudge which the poet bears against his time. The reason for this grudge may be that poets not only want to make poetry, to enjoy the consciousness of a poetic kind of being, they want the experience of poetic living to be realized in the lines of their poetry, poetry and life at times to be one in the writing of the poetry. It is the sense that he has been exiled from being the fisherman who symbolizes the being-creating fusion that is the bitterness in Yeats. Poets do not want to be "Intellectuals."

The bitterness of which I am speaking takes the form, in Lawrence, of rage against what he calls "cerebral" writing, and the program he set himself for being himself in all he wrote. "I write with everything vague— plenty of fire underneath, but, like bulbs in the ground, only shadowy flowers that must be beaten and sustained, for another spring" (letter to Edward Garnett, 29 January 1914). Lawrence—if any modern writer— is organic, but that is both his strength and his weakness. There is something about his work, even at its best, which is like material splitting at the seams. And the split is caused, I think, by the separation of his view of what is life from his practice of literature. His philosophy of living through the senses and through instincts suppressed in the modern age leaves little room for art, because it is a revolt against the aesthetic consciousness, a return to a more primitive poetic activity. It is an attitude which can be preached but which cannot attain an expression in which the famous Laurentian sense of life and full artistic awareness resolved in satisfactory form are fused. Thus, in certain passages about the dark gods, phallic consciousness, sex, and the like, Lawrence gives the impression that the life expressed does not lie in the art realized but in the physical body or the instinctual life of the reader. Sometimes the printed page, as it were, sacrificially or sacramentally represents the physical or the instinctual and sexual body of Lawrence himself. He makes it clear that by phallic con-

[27]

sciousness he means only his own particular variety of blood consciousness and sexual feeling, and that he disapproves of behavior which does not accord with the models he lays down.

Thus, although there is modern organic poetry, it is the result of a fusion which seems forced, and this is felt in a cerain jarring quality in the technique and form. In a way different from Lawrence, but which leads me to think that he would have preferred Lawrence—as he did Walt Whitman—to many of his contemporaries, Gerard Manley Hopkins is organic; his poetry seems always the result of the fusion of the external experience acting directly upon his sensibility and producing language and form. But the identification with external circumstances is either the result of deliberately willed involution with nature—what Hopkins called "inscape"—or of great anguish. One may merely prefer the poetry of Hopkins to the literary flow of Tennyson—and, still more, of Swinburne—yet the willedness makes for unbearable strain, and the suffering seems at times the perverse result of Hopkins' violation of his own poetic nature. Just as the organic in Wordsworth seems the kineticism of muscular movement across a childhood scene returned to by the poet, producing a kinetic poetry, so with Hopkins there is the kineticism of willed visual concentration, grinding despair.

We have the sense, then, that modern circumstances have set up a screen between nature and man so that the harmonious relationship realized in organic poetry, in which the soul sees itself reflected in the physical environment, is prevented. The only way of return to the being-creating fusion is through spiritual or physical violence, tearing down the screen and forcing the inner sensibility into contact with the external.

Hence, it seems that intellectual awareness of the situation which has set up the barrier is necessary for poetry to develop language and forms which do not appear to be the result of a forced juxtaposition of inner and outer situations:

> *Between the conception*
> *And the creation*
> *Between the emotion*
> *And the response*
> *Falls the Shadow.*

What I call "Intellectualized" is the work in which consciousness of the task undertaken, the means employed, the necessary strategy, dominate the writing. Instead of the old being-creating thee is the poetic-critical fusion.

Imagination Means Individuation

THE ATTITUDES OF MODERN POETS cannot be understood, even in the case of Eliot, simply as their being a reaction against Romanticism and a return to tradition and othodoxy. On the surface it would, of course, seem that the most obvious characteristic of the movement in poetry initiated by Hulme, Pound, and Eliot early in the present century was a revolt against Romantic standards. And it is true that the great bloc made by the Romantics (shutting out the view of everything beyond the early nineteenth century except the highest peaks of English poetry—Shakespeare, Chaucer, and Milton) has been removed. Today, students realize that Shelley, Keats, and Byron were extraordinary men with extraordinary gifts living in an extraordinary time, but they know, also, that these poets had little time in which to mature, and that the collected works of Shelley are a wild, exotic, and unweeded garden.

With the Romantic bloc removed, words concretely used, metaphors that are coherent and not vague have, as it were, surged forward, passed through the undisciplined Romantic lines, and joined hands with present poetry. Marvell, Dryden, and Pope have become accessible to us in a way that perhaps they were not to Victorian readers. *I read Othello's visage in his mind:* a generation that began by learning the calm and beauty realized in the surface of seventeenth- and eighteenth-century poetry, stayed to prefer that order to the Romantic disorder.

However, this cutting of Romantic poetry down to size did not lead to the new classicism which T. E. Hulme predicted in his *Speculations*. What it did initiate was a revolution in method, in technique, in spreading the idea that writing poetry was deliberate and conscious work and not a matter of entering into an effluvial state of self-intoxication. Yet against this picture of return to a pre-Romantic consciousness of the intellectual problems of writing poetry, we have to bear in mind that, by and large, the criticism of the Augustan poets by the Romantics has, with certain qualifications, been accepted by the anti-Romantic moderns, perhaps on the grounds of its *historic necessity* rather than its critical justice but accepted nevertheless. When Eliot retracted some of his early attack on Milton, he gave as his excuse that, as a young man, it had been necessary for him to attack Milton for the sake of the development of his own poetry, just as it had been a poetic necessity for Wordsworth to attack Pope.

So we are confronted with the paradox that, although there has been a reaction against the Romantics and back toward the poets who preceded them, nevertheless, the same poet-critics who made this revolt have taken over the subjective view of the imagination which was Romantic. Joyce, Yeats (in his later work), Eliot, and Pound combine critical consciousness in the *act* of writing with instinctive subjective consciousness in their use of material from dreams, as well as in their fragmentariness, obscurity, mysteriousness, and the like. They are objective in being extremely aware of what they want to say and how to say it; they are subjective in their realization that everything said has to be reinvented from the deepest and most isolated center of individual imagination. They are aware of the importance of contemporary idiom; but they are also aware of the greater importance of the magic of language which is "rich and strange."

There could not be a return to eighteenth-century classicism—to the idea of the unified intellectual culture of an elite, exercising reason to reconcile science, God, and the aristocracy, and sublimating the arguments in transparent poetry. The Romantics are of our modern world, and modern poetry comes out of their situation. When we uphold Pope against the Romantics we are, after all, only expressing the view that Byron also expressed—despising the works of himself and his contemporaries, and advocating Pope but having to be Byron.

There has been talk, on and off, ever since T. E. Hulme's *Speculations*, of a new classicism. Hulme thought that a movement of Cubists and Vorticists in painting and of Imagists in poetry could be founded on a synthesis between the tradition of pre-Renaissance nonindividualist Byzantine art and the cold abstract forms of the dehumanized modern age of machinery. But classical revivals cannot be based on dubious historic analogies. Interpreted into political action, Hulme's wish to put the clock back to an authoritarian age, indifferent to human values, was Fascism. His aesthetic ideas became economic theory and Fascist ideology in the *Cantos* of his admirer, Ezra Pound. The obvious objection to a classical revival is that there is no unity of outlook in our modern age, divided between science and the humanities. The only unity we can have is of a kind forced upon us by state-directed politics. A willed and forced modern parody of classicism is that branch of propagandist advertising extended into art, which is called social realism.

So, in a civilization split in its allegiances between scientific scepticism, specialization, and utilitarianism and the surviving religious and cultural traditions—more powerful, these, than is generally admitted—there can be no classical revival. What we have instead, is the setting up of outposts of orthodoxy and dogma in the modern waste land. Eliot, Auden, and others have established fortresses of past tradition, reimagined, reinvented in the contemporary idiom of their poetry. But just because terms like tradition, orthodoxy, and dogma are employed, we should not confuse the comparatively isolated position of the orthodox with a time when whole societies were orthodoxies. A dogma today remains sectarian in a society of sects, religious and secular. Orthodoxy today is not that of society but of the orthodox only.

I am here considering literature and not religion. For I well understand that from a religious standpoint it is not very important whether there are few believers or many. Faith may burn more intensely in the day of outcasts than in that of complacent establishments. But for literature, the question whether the religious symbolism and tradition of poets correspond to those in the minds of their readers does matter. For nonbelieving readers, I do not think that there is a great difference between the orthodox symbolism of writers like Eliot and Auden and the heterodoxy of Rilke or the eclectic religion of Yeats, as realized in their poetry. Moreover, I think this is recognized by Eliot in his poetic practice. For he does not write so much as one conforming to a doctrine already present and accepted in the mind of his reader, as like one who invents (just as much as Rilke or Yeats) his symbols and values.

There is every difference, of course, between religious faith and poetic imagination. But the modern poet may have to reinvent his faith as poetic imagination; and so to the common reader the difference between the dogma of Eliot and the private religions of Rilke or Yeats may not seem apparent or to matter to the poetry.

This brings us back to the central role of the imagination in modern as in Romantic poetry. In a world of fragmented values, the imagination cannot illustrate accepted doctrines, cannot refer to symbolic meanings already recognized by the reader, symbols of the faith he believes in and imbibed with his education. Everything has to be reinvented, as it were, from the beginning, and anew in each work. Every position has to be *imagined* in the poem. The imagining cannot be left to the social environment.

But if there are not ceremonies, symbols, sacraments, generally accepted by the community, within the ritual of living—if society offers no face but the mere machinery of receiving work and giving pay, and providing amusement and distractions; and if beyond this there lurk only the life-or-death, promising-or-threatening abstract hopes and fears of the machines— then, nonetheless, the artist has to find referents of human consciousness on which to work. These referents are inevitably the elemental qualities of the individual's experience of life—his inescapable awareness, after all, that he is alive and situated in a time and place—his hopes and fears, his loves and hates. He is capable of being shown of what consciousness consists.

There is in much modern literature an evocation of compensatory depths in individual human life. Everyone carries round an infinity, if not in his head, then in his sex. If his thoughts are cupboard-size, his dreams, nevertheless, open onto prairies, constellations. Art invokes the subconscious world to counterbalance the conscious results of materialism. The most potent and awesome lesson of Joyce's *Ulysses* and *Finnegans Wake* is that an eyelid, open or shut to let in the light of consciousness, the dark of sleep, can open out in every direction into memories which, through chains of association, would traverse the whole past and future of humanity. Sometimes Lawrence seems convinced that the forces of the unconscious released by the sexual act might transform the whole world, make men and women become gods instead of being social units.

It is this appeal to forces stronger than those in conscious individuality, but which yet *are* the individual and of which he can be made conscious, that writers as opposed as Lawrence and Joyce and movements as divergent as futurism, dadaism, surrealism, and existentialism yet have in common. Freud, Jung, and other psychologists have, of course, provided a theoretical background for this literature, which could hardly have been written without them.

In times when there are no generally shared religious or societal interpretations of experience, the artist may take over the task of inventing his own referents, or of reinforcing past ones as though they were reinvented for his poetic purposes. There is the idea of a burden, a task, a pressure of disparate outer things seeking to realize themselves as inner significance, running through the history of poetry during the past hundred and more years. One may, of course, resent this burden, on the grounds that it puts responsibility of a too vast and altogether too public and impersonal kind on the artist, who can only retain his integrity by limiting his experience within the scope of that which he can personalize. The objection to Shelley's "we must imagine that which we know" is on these grounds. A history of poetry during the past hundred years and more could be written that would relate it to swings between the pole of the idea of the imagination as a task imposed, and that of it as strictly limited to the poet's most confined personal awareness.

As so often in such controversies, there is no real contradiction here—for in fact nothing is artistically significant unless it has become personalized. But there are, nonetheless, pressures and tensions from the outside life upon the inner consciousness. Social conscience can easily work a destructive effect upon artistic conscience, which is not a duty toward society at all but a duty of being conscious as an individual and as an artist. And those who are aware of this danger may insist too much that consciousness can only be about things that are private.

The ideal and often evoked task for the poet in society is to personalize in his work the greatest possible amount and intensity of interest outside his private concerns. A world of external impersonal forces must be sacrificially reinvented as the poet's inner personal world, so that, for his readers, the impersonal modern world may be personalized in poetry. To avoid misunderstanding, I repeat that I do not mean that a poet has to become a public figure or that—to use Keats' phrase—the shadow of public life must fall across his work. What I am concerned with is his awareness of a contemporary situation which affects personal relations and art itself, and which is different from past situations.

The great example of an attempt to personalize the contemporary situation was, of course, Walt Whitman's, especially in *Song of Myself*. Walt Whitman took upon himself the task of imagining the America of his day and of seeking to invent in his poetry the geographical and historical concept of America which his contemporaries and future generations of Americans might themselves realize in their feelings and attitudes. In order to accomplish this, Whitman had not only to invent a kind of poetry different from European models, but he had to become America, as America had, in a sense, in his own imagination, to become Whitman. A great deal of his poetry is about this process, about how Whitman became the wounded of the Civil War, how the continent entered into and absorbed the consciousness of Whitman (just as in *Finnegans Wake* the landscape becomes the consciousness of Joyce's dreamer). Whitman summarizes himself:

Immense have been the preparations for me,
Faithful and friendly the arms that have help'd me.

Cycles ferried my cradle, rowing and rowing like cheerful boatmen;
For room to me stars kept aside in their own rings;
They sent influences to look after what was to hold me.
Before I was born out of my mother, generations guided me;
My embryo has never been torpid—nothing could overlay it.

For it the nebula cohered to an orb,
The long slow strata piled to rest it on,
Vast vegetables gave it sustenance,
Monstrous sauroids transported it in their mouths, and
    deposited it with care.

All forces have been steadily employ'd to complete and delight me;
Now on this spot I stand with my robust Soul.

Everything has to become thus personal and individuated to be imagined, because there is no such thing as a public imagination. Imagination means individuation. What is imagined may be a world as large as that of Shakespeare or Dickens; but it is imagined by one person, the writer. And it becomes part of the life of one person, the reader.

The kind of communication that is art rests on the truth that individuation is the basic pattern of all experiencing—that everyone, in his view of everything outside him, in his knowledge of past and present, in his relations with other people, and even in what he has read, makes, and is, his own world. He may be influenced by others, he may be unoriginal and be scarcely conscious of having an identity separate from that of colleagues or tribe, but the fact remains that he is irreducibly himself, filling a body and occupying a time and space that are no one's but his own and perceiving things through his sense organs that are no one else's. The "truth" of poetry is that it discourses on this just assumption that poet and reader are unique. Every poet begins again from the beginning that is himself, and outside experience meets in the center that is his unique sensibility.

Poetry is, then, not a cooperative effort leading to collective results, as is science, in which the personal contribution becomes absorbed into the body of collected impersonal knowledge and the personal quality of the scientist disappears. There is, of course, in each country, a "sum" of poetry which consists of all the poems written in that language; and they add up to more than any poem or poems. But, supposing that the total poems in a language could be signified by the figure 100, then it is a total in which each figure remains, as it were, separate, a sum of 1 and 1 and 1, each retaining its uniqueness though a fraction of, and contributing to, the whole. Through the fusion of the imagination of the writer with that of the reader, the reader is able to hear with the ears, see through the eyes, and feel with the feelings of the writer, the world which becomes that of both. This is possible because the outward forms and techniques of art imitate— as the leaf the seed—the inner mode of perception of the poet, a person, experiencing through his unique mind and body the world outside himself. The poet is writing as one person for the reader reading as one person.

A situation which holds true of poetry in all its communication is that expressed in *A Shropshire Lad* by Housman, dramatizing to the person he loves—who certainly will not understand—that ideal communication which is simply that of one life situated, speaking to another also situated:

> From far, from eve and morning
>   And yon twelve-winded sky,
> The stuff of life to knit me
>   Blew hither: here am I.
>
> Now—for a breath I tarry
>   Nor yet disperse apart—
> Take my hand quick and tell me,
>   What have you in your heart.
>
> Speak now, and I will answer;
>   How shall I help you, say;
> Ere to the wind's twelve quarters
>   I take my endless way.

It is extremely important, I think, to insist that the poetic imagination is centripetal, a bringing together of experiences from a circumference which could theoretically be enlarged to include all pasts and presents, all things

[34]

known and experienced, into the center of the artist's individual sensibility where they are the projected patterns which communicate that consciousness to readers.

The view has been put forward recently by C. P. Snow, in a famous and much-debated essay, that there are today two cultures, a scientific and a literary. It is clear that what Sir Charles means by "culture" in this context are, on the one hand the ideas and *mores* of scientists and those, on the other, of writers. He is concerned with what is being discovered and what is being imagined. Sir Charles reproaches scientists for their ignorance of literature and the literary figures for their ignorance of science. He wants there to be bridges between the so-called two cultures. He tries to apportion blame equally to both sides in the alleged controversy, but it is evident that his sympathies are really with the scientists. He enters into their reasons for not appreciating the poets. He does not enter into the reasons of the poets for not appreciating the scientists. For he bases his whole case on ignorance and knowledge. The scientists do not *know* literature and the men of letters do not know science. Put like this, obviously the writers are the more to blame, for science is knowledge, whereas literature is the imagining of that which can be imagined. On grounds of knowledge, the scientists are not to be blamed for not knowing works of the imagination, since from their point of view they offer little to know. The members of the literary culture have, in his view, ignored a renaissance taking place in science; all that the scientists, on their side, appear to have ignored are the medieval ideas of antiprogressive men of letters.

As a thesis, a good deal of this seems open to dispute. I happen to know that the favorite reading of one of the most eminent physicists, J. D. Bernal, is *Finnegans Wake*. In itself this may not be statistically significant. Yet one can see why a physicist might be interested in Joyce, whose novels are just as much an invention of the modern mind as is a jet aircraft, whose technique has resemblances to work in the laboratory, and whose intelligence expresses a new kind of sensibility. It would be crude, surely, of scientists to think that novels to be scientific have to be about scientists or about matters of social administration, and poems, about social progress. A scientist would surely agree that if literature is scientific it is nevertheless dealing with special kinds of material and uses special techniques. An argument defending poetry, on the ground that poets employ extremely subtle and complex techniques for expressing the psychology of individuals, has been put forward by I. A. Richards, and it should have been considered by C. P. Snow if he wished to avoid the charge that what he really meant was that literature should reflect scientific progress and so earn the interest of scientists.

Sir Charles raises important points which have not, perhaps, so much to do with culture as with the education of children who later become scientists or writers, but he blurs the distinction between the world as viewed

[35]

by science and the world as viewed by poetic imagination. Restricting even the difference to the level of Sir Charles' debate (that the scientists are progressives and the writers reactionaries), it remains true that science is concerned with the extension of the resources of materials and power which can be put to general use, while literature is concerned with the meaning that individual life has in the world in which these resources have been made available.

It may be true that certain modern writers—poets, especially—have shown too great antipathy to the beneficial aspects of science. Though the reason they have done so is because they are quite rightly concerned not with science but with the modern world which is so largely the result of science. It is a world in which past values have been fragmented, in which the constructive powers of science are balanced by its powers of destruction, in which the forces of human personality have broken down, and men and women have come to think of themselves as "social units." But to blame scientists, in their disinterested pursuit of knowledge, for all this would be as unwarranted as to blame writers for delivering their warnings against progress. On the whole, it would seem that for the so-called literary culture to be critical of the so-called scientific is right. As the most interesting poet of World War I, Wilfred Owen, wrote in the preface to his poems: "All a poet can do to-day is warn."

By a literary culture we should mean, I think, the poems, plays, novels—and perhaps also works in new media and forms, such as radio and television and science fiction—which, ideally, should imagine the whole experience of living, should treat the past as well as the present as a single whole within individual consciousness. The literary culture is essentially critical of the contemporary world, which is the result of the scientific. This criticism may be expressed explicitly in critical works or imaginatively in poetic ones. It keeps alive the sense of the past as living thoughts and feelings crystalized, and in this way it judges present living by the realities of past life. Thus, in America today there are traditions still vital within the work of classic American writers, which, as it were, stand in perpetual court of judgment over what is today American life. Modern American literature seems, moreover, to indicate that everyone is not happy in a civilization largely devoted to flooding consumers with consumer goods.

Sir Charles Snow attacks the representatives of the "literary culture" (he means Ezra Pound and T. S. Eliot) for their hostility to progressive ideas, and he argues that to take sides against progress today means letting large numbers of people starve. But even while he is making this attack, the moral bias of it does not come out of the methods of science, which are conducive equally to killing large numbers of people and to feeding them. "Progress" is one of those ideas with roots in primitive Christianity, humanism, and the French Revolution, which form one aspect of a long debate that is an important part of Victorian and twentieth-century literature. Scientists who support progress do not belong to a special scientific culture, but to that of Dickens, Shaw, and Wells.

Science today is concerned with research and technology; the poetic imagination is concerned with testing the values of the modern world, which is so largely the result of science as experienced good or evil, by the standard of the past tradition relived in the consciousness of the artist, realized in his work, and judged by his reader. Progress produces material benefits, but it is only through the alive intelligence of the imagination that these can be related to significant values. And although the great material needs of the world can and should be satisfied by progress, there is the great spiritual danger of judging individual lives as units in the progressive society, that is, as social units which ought to be statistically happier and to live statistically better lives because statistically they are better fed. But perhaps a parallel problem with undernourishment is that people are not automatically better or even happier as a result of social improvements. For example, it is notorious that in England the real benefits accomplished by the Welfare State have produced an unprecedented spiritual malaise. If there were danger of stopping progress as a result of T. S. Eliot's "reactionary" attitude towards it, there might be justification for the charge that the supporters of the literary culture are in favor of taking potential bread out of the mouths of the starving. But since this is not the case, they are surely right in drawing attention to the spiritual crisis which results from beneficial materialism.

Though I do not agree with the formula of the "two cultures," I think that within the "literary culture" itself, it may well be just to criticize poets for their ignorance of the great advances made by science. This criticism leads back to the problem of the imagination. For there are examples enough to show—the effect on Coleridge's poetry of his delvings into abstract philosophy is one—that the poetic imagination is harmed by absorbing more intellectual knowledge than it can digest. The poet can use no more knowledge than he can transform into his poetry, the novelist no more than he can make the behavior and dialogue of realized action and characters.

What writers may fruitfully know is that which they can experience with their sensibility. So it is not so important that they should know the second law of thermodynamics as that they should perceive the subtle changes effected in the rhythm of language by the environment resulting from inventions and its influence on human behavior and modes of feeling. It is not scientific knowledge but its effects which become part of the experience of modern life. Joyce, Eliot, and Lawrence certainly reflect in their works the results of science. Even in his own novels, C. P. Snow creates fiction about the results of science and bureaucracy, not about scientific theories and business management. And if one were to defend the two-dimensional characters in these novels, one would argue that these embodiments of ideas and petty ambitions are studies of the effect on human beings of working in laboratories, colleges, and government departments. It may be that without knowing it, with his imagination Snow creates a picture which is critical of progress, and that as an artist he agrees with T. S. Eliot, whom as a critic he dismisses as reactionary, that "we are the hollow men."

Shakespeare did not have to know the philosophical and scientific theorizing of his time to reflect the passionate individualism of the Renaissance. Dante, of course, was immensely learned in the theory of the universe of his age. The knowledge of his time was of a kind which interpreted the whole of existence within the unity of a single view of of life. Knowledge and imagination were then one and the same. It is possible, of course, that the present revolution in science might arrive at the point where analytic and statistical inquiry broke down, and the behavior of infinitesimally small impulses, particles of energy, appeared entirely accidental, and their interpretation was inevitably subjective to the scientist. In that event, the poetic imagination would link up with the scientific, and perhaps we would, at the end of an immensely long journey, return to a culture based on the unity of logic and imagination. Saint-John Perse pointed out in his Nobel Prize acceptance discourse at Stockholm: "Le mystère est commun. Et la grande aventure de l'esprit poétique ne le cède en rien aux ouvertures dramatiques de la science moderne. Des astronomes ont pu s'affoler d'une théorie de l'univers en expansion: il n'est pas moins d'expansion dans l'infini moral de l'homme— cet univers."

But visions of modern experience of life seen as a whole seem to depend on the imaginative interpretation of the forces that are the results of science. And in the twentieth century, the standpoint from which it has been possible for poetic imaginations to envisage modern life as a whole seems to be that of life viewed as tragedy, a position made more convincing by our catastrophic modern history. The modern works in which life has been seen steadily and whole are the pessimistic poetry of Hardy, the apocalyptic *Waste Land,* and the dancing over the graves of the dead of the later Yeats.

The poetic imagination is, then, individual, and the ideal task of modern poetry, as it was envisaged by the Romantics, and as it haunts the artistic conscience still today, is to imagine the modern experience of life through the sensibility of the individual poet and as a whole. The history of modern literature is one of writers approaching and withdrawing from this challenge.

When the withdrawal occurs because the poet feels that his talents or interests or view of poetry should be limited to what he can best deal with, there is no cause for protest. The concept of a great task like a public duty should not be set threateningly over art.

So the use of the phrase "the two cultures" blurs the distinction between two different things by treating them as if each were the same kind of thing. The idea that the literary culture is opposed to, or that it should be complementary to, the scientific culture, and that intellectual life is split into these two halves, suggests one of those false dichotomies, like "personal issues" and "newspaper issues," which today bedevil intellectual debate. Adding to the confusion is the difficulty attached to defining the word "culture" itself. Sometimes Snow uses this as though he means a center of contemporary awareness, sometimes as if he means the symptomatic behavior of a group. One might say that scientific workers show certain dispositions, develop certain propensities—a liking for gadgets, for example, and an indifference to modern poetry: this makes them a culture. And from the same sociological viewpoint, writers have traits in common which make them a culture: some of them smoke pipes, wear tweeds, and pretend to be countrymen or farmers.

But if the two cultures are in competition it is because each of them has claims to interpret the significant life of the time. From this point of view the characteristic of the literary culture is the attempt of writers to create forms that express the significance of life which they have both experienced and imagined. What is so expressed can be summed up in the phrase: "how it is to be alive in a given set of circumstances." Imagination is that which enables the poet to enter into situations which extend beyond himself, into other lives, other times, other places.

Thus, a Wordsworth, a Blake, or a Lawrence, while being himself—and thus representing in his work the mode by which experience is felt, through his individual sensibility—is also occupied with interpreting into artistic forms the effects on individual life of what are, in the widest sense, contemporary conditions, which he measures against the imagined past and his appreciation of the potentialities of life.

Obviously, the functions of science have been quite different from this, and are in no way competing with or parallel to it. Historically, scientists have been preoccupied with accumulating knowledge, theories, techniques, instruments, machinery. It has been the understanding of science that knowledge is pursued for its own sake, and that its discoveries and inventions are handed over to those who use them without the scientist having responsibility beyond the research which has gone into them, the validity of the experiments by which they have been proven or tested. The scientist is responsible to a kind of truth which is not human in its concern for its effect upon human beings.

The individual scientist uses the knowledge and instruments which have been put at his disposal by past and present other scientists. He does not have a vital concern with the past of science, because there is no question but that science is progressive. The most recent stage of development of any branch of science is an advance on previous ones. The new discovery absorbs into itself past discoveries—unless there is question of an error which has to be uncovered and corrected.

Literature is not in this way progressive. On the contrary, poets are dogged with the feeling that earlier poetry may be better not only than theirs but better than anything they are able to do: and since they regard poetry as in some respect the measure of the individual condition in its time, the fact they feel that conditions undermine their talents bears witness, also, against the life of this time.

U.S. GOVERNMENT PRINTING OFFICE:1961